Return to the Mother
A Lover's Handbook

Other Books by Red Hawk

Poetry

Journey of the Medicine Man (August House, 1983)
The Sioux Dog Dance (Cleveland State University, 1991)
The Way of Power (Hohm Press, 1996)
The Art of Dying (Hohm Press, 1999)
Wreckage With A Beating Heart (Hohm Press, 2005)
Raven's Paradise, winner: Bright Hill Press Poetry Prize (2010)
The Indian Killer (Anjaneya Press, 2013), signed and numbered,
    limited edition
Mother Guru: Savitri Love Poems (Hohm Press, 2014)

Non-fiction

*Self Observation: The Awakening of Conscience: An Owner's
    Manual* (Hohm Press, 2009)
*Self Remembering: The Path to Non-Judgmental Love: A Practi-
    tioner's Manual* (Hohm Press, 2015)

Return to the Mother
A Lover's Handbook

¹¹/₂₀₁₇

Poems of Self Remembering
and Self Observation
Inspired by Lao Tsu's
Tao Te Ching

RED HAWK

Hohm Press
Chino Valley, Arizona

Cover Art: Doris Kreickhaus. Original watercolor on rice paper. Used with permission of the estate of Doris Martha Kessler Krieckhaus.

Cover Design: Becky Fulker, Kubera Book Design, Prescott, Arizona

Interior Design and Layout: Becky Fulker, Kubera Book Design, Prescott, Arizona

Library of Congress Control Number: 2017936494

ISBN: 978-1-942493-30-3

Hohm Press
P.O. Box 4410
Chino Valley, AZ 86323
800-381-2700
http://www.hohmpress.com

This book was printed in the U.S.A. on recycled, acid-free paper using soy ink.

Dedication

Sum Ergo Amo ("I Am Therefore I Love")
Te Dominus Amat ("The Love of God")

For Mister Lee: Adoro te Devote;
for Yogi Ramsuratkumar.

for Chandrika: Te Amo, Te Adoro.

for Little Wind & Rain Drop;
for the Grandsons: Iain, Jett, Jayce.

Contents

---

* The number after each title refers to the Sutra from *Tao Te Ching* that inspires each poem.

Author's Preface

On our way to a mountain cabin in Ashe County, North Carolina, Chandrika and I stopped for lunch in Abingdon, Virginia. After lunch we went to a small bookstore-coffee shop (more coffee than books). I went to the poetry section, which was two shelves of mostly local poets. There I discovered a broken-spined hardback book by Wayne Dyer entitled *Change Your Thoughts, Change Your Life: Living the Wisdom of the Tao.* I have long admired the *Tao Te Ching*, the book of ancient Wisdom by Lao Tsu; for many years my worn copy has been by my bedside.

I opened Wayne Dyer's book and found that he had taken versions of the *Tao* from ten different translations and selected the ones from each version which he favored, first giving the translation of the *Tao*, and then following with two-three pages of commentary and exercises. Various lines of Lao Tsu's text suggested poem titles to me.

This led to an outpouring of poems, suggested by various lines from this new assorted version of the *Tao Te Ching*. So I am indebted to Wayne Dyer for his very fine selection of versions, various translations, and for the inspiration which it provided me in the creation of this book of poems. I have used mainly his selections here; where I have used other translations, they are noted following the title; please see the bibliography.

Each title is a quote from the *Tao*, followed in parentheses by the number of the sutra. This volume is a companion to the two volumes which preceded it: *Self Observation: The Awakening of Conscience. An Owner's Manual*; and *Self Remembering: The Path to Non-Judgmental Love. A Practitioner's Manual* (both from Hohm Press).

Taken together, these three volumes form a trilogy which examines the spiritual practice of self remembering/self observation. They owe their inspiration and creation to Mister Lee Lozowick, my Beloved Spiritual Master, whose suggestion it was that I write the first volume. His ever-present help and support have sustained me in this long project. My Beloved wife Chandrika has provided invaluable help and feedback throughout, as has Regina Sara Ryan, editor extraordinaire. *Te Amo*.

It is an honor, a privilege, right and just that this work is a collaboration with these women artists, whose work moves me, enhances the poems, and extends their meanings; with all my Heart I thank the following artists for their contributions to this project: Clelia Lewis, her mother Doris Kreickhaus, Sally Sunlight Roach, Denise Incao, Michelle Meaux, Jocelyn Del Rio and Simona Sasarman.

Red Hawk

Prologue

"All under heaven..."

**"All under heaven have a common beginning.
This beginning is the Mother of the world."** (52)

All of us have the same Mother, therefore
we are all brothers and sisters,
only one race, the Human race, all

one family. But this is cliché, we have
all heard this from the TV preachers
before they ask us to send money.

What good do such words do?
Our Mother has no words, She is
Silence, She is the present, here-

now. To be here-now, in this body,
is to return to Our Mother,
relaxed, soft, open, receptive:

kind.
Kindness is the nature of Our Mother,
Non-Judgmental Love is Her Being, and

we are Her children, made in Her image.

Return to the Mother

1

"Ever desireless, one can see the mystery." (1)

Desire is like a poorly constructed
Earthen dam:
its breech is inevitable, and

once it is breeched, all the villages,
the fields, the farms, the cattle,
the crops, the women and children

are swept away.
What is left then is barren waste,
wreckage with a broken heart;

shame follows as the shadow
follows a man all of his life.
He who wishes for real change

watches his desires like a Hawk
watching its prey; unlike the Hawk,
he does not seize, nor does he fly away:

he remains steady, vigilant, still, impersonal.

2

"The name that can be named is not the eternal name." (1. ii)

By naming we are cast out of the garden,
we lose our innocence; naming
is eating the fruit of the tree

of knowledge of good and evil;
it creates the fatal dichotomy:
namer and named,

this and that, I and thou,
like and dislike, good
and evil; all judgment

is born of naming. Naming
is the mind's strategy
to avoid relationship; it is

a recoil into fear. The present
is unnamable: neither this
nor that. Some land

is too wild to be named.*

---

*   Last line inspired by Sandy Longhorn's poem "Having Been Begotten" (*The Girlhood Book of Prairie Myths*, Jacar Press, 2013).

3

"When the work is done, it is forgotten." (2)

"We commissioned the (Andy) Goldsworthy outdoor wall
with the tree embedded in it.
He built a layer of a wall

upon a wall that existed.
Over the course of time
the tree has rotted, and

this year the wall has collapsed.
We are not supposed to rebuild the wall
because you have to have faith

that future generations will lay
their wall on top of our wall, as we've
laid ours on top of the past...

You can't move it,
you can't sell it,
it has no economic value, and

it's falling down."

(*Source:* Sherry and Joel Mallin, Pound Ridge, N.Y. Quoted in *Art News:* Summer
2013, 85.)

4

"So the sage lives openly with apparent duality…" (2. ii)

The mind as we know it is a binary computer,
thus by its very nature it is dual and
therefore sees every phenomenon in dualistic terms:

good-bad or like-dislike. This does not mean
the mind is the enemy, this is dualistic itself,
a dichotomy: "me" and "it—the enemy."

Mind is a computer, a logic-machine, a useful
and necessary tool, never meant to be
identified with as the self, the master of the house;

the practice of self remembering/self observation
is given to work with the mind,
to tame and train it, not to defeat it:

to steady, clarify, simplify and re-order it, so
it operates with great precision and efficiency,
quiet and alert, waiting to be called upon for data,

a faithful dog, responding to a kind, intelligent master.

5

**"Under heaven all can see beauty as beauty,
only because there is ugliness."** (2. iii)

Physical beauty is finest when it admits a flaw,
whose contrast makes the beauty greater
than if it were a lone, untroubled jewel;

the eye needs such contrast; it is easy to fool.
The mind which beholds beauty is both creator
and is itself made more beautiful by its awe,

before which it cannot think, but only admire.
Great beauty does not boast or make a show,
it has no need of advertisement, is understated

and by this reticence is its allure created;
the purest modesty arouses the deepest desire.
It needs no artifice, no paint or artificial glow.

Beauty steals the heart because it dies;
in its impermanence, its greatest attraction lies.
All beauty comes from the Mother, returns:

ashes to ashes, all that has form burns.

6

"The sage governs by emptying minds and hearts." (3)

Mind and heart are empty vessels, filled
by life with fear, which translates
in our world as desire.

Once innocence is lost,
we know the body will die, thus
we are afraid because we identify ourselves

as the body; if we think of the Soul or Being,
we identify it as separate from ourselves.
This dichotomy is not useful: the body functions

as an Objective feedback mechanism to orient
the Being in the present; once it is rooted there,
the mind becomes an empty vessel and

the heart, like a stream after Spring rain,
flows steadily with a love both Conscious
and non-judgmental: the first stage is

the Being's adoration of the body.

7

"The Tao is empty but inexhaustible." (4)

The wise do not horde,
why should they?
The source of their wealth

cannot be exhausted,
emptiness overflows
with goodness; form

gives way, is impermanent,
returns to emptiness.
Have you seen the body

once the Being departs?
Then you have seen emptiness,
which gave rise to the form.

The wise do not cling to the form,
but remain always in the
inexhaustible emptiness; they do not

grieve over-long when the form vanishes.

8

"The sage is not sentimental; hold on to the center." (5)

Sentiment is always from the past,
never present,
never here-now, thus

it is fear-based, born
of the desire to cling to the past;
its inevitable end is sorrow.

The wise remain with attention
centered in the body, moving
neither towards stray thoughts nor

towards inflamed emotions, steady
and without desire, observing
as thought and emotion move

first this way, then that:
between this and that, between
yesterday and tomorrow, nothing

takes root; thus, Nothing remains.

9

**"The valley spirit never dies;
It is the woman, primal mother."** (6) (Gia-Fu Feng)

It is called primal because It is
prime, first, It cannot be named,
cannot be known,

only experienced, only lived,
a present-phenomenon only, therefore
Death can never find it.

It is called the Woman, Primal Mother
because It is the gateway through which
all life passes and takes form,

the hollow bowl which fills
with water, the eternal emptiness
from which all life arises,

the Mother of creation:
rest in Her and you rest in peace,
for Her love will never fail; stray

and you become the hunted.

10

"The spirit that never dies is called the mysterious feminine." (6. ii)

The Feminine, the source of all life,
is a mystery: the Masculine is logic,
reason, mathematical, but

the Feminine is the passion of
the Sacred Heart of Mercy and
the heart has reasons which reason

cannot comprehend, therefore
the Feminine is called mysterious.
In order to bond with Her,

I must lose my mind and
come to my senses;
reason can only come as far as

the gate, but to pass through into
the unknown Feminine is unreasonable;
he who passes through is called

Valley-Dweller, Womb-Guardian, Husband.

11

**"The gateway to the mysterious female
is called the root of creation."** (6. iii)

Oh men, dear men, broken like parched straw
in the field after a bad storm, do you see
that the Feminine is the source

of all creation? Therefore, all creation
longs to bond, to merge, with the Feminine force;
it cannot be found outside of you,

it cannot be controlled by you,
it cannot be dominated by you:
the urge to control is a sickness

brought about by fear. Presence and attention
serve the Feminine force: brought to the root
and resting there, they create; held captive

in the mind they destroy. The Feminine
awaits you in Stillness within. Surrender
to the Mother and order is restored. Then,

everything is under Her control.

12

**"[The sage] stays a witness to life,
so he endures."** (7) (Star)

The Sage is not a person,
it is a condition,
a state of Consciousness,

a present-phenomenon only,
therefore the Sage cannot die.
A precious few

have animated that state of Consciousness;
they are called Sages, Wise Ones, Guru.
The state which they animate is called

Witness Consciousness, in which presence
and attention remain still and centered,
not captured by thought or emotion,

taking no position regarding the arising
of phenomena. This allows
the true nature of the Being to manifest as

Non-Judgmental Love: It alone endures.

13

**"One who lives in accordance with nature...
moves in harmony with the present moment."** (8)

The slightest movement away from the present
is fear: what the fool calls "me-myself"
is an imaginary creation, a strategic defense

to avoid living in harmony with the present;
thus "myself" is inevitably unharmonious,
out of alignment, out of relationship

with love, which is the present.
See how the water, that softest and
most yielding of substances, that

Feminine force of life, always seeks
to flow downhill, around obstacles,
the easeful, harmonious way. This

is how one who is in accordance with nature
lives: relaxed in the body, surrendered
into the present, the here-now of love;

no fight, no blame, Just This.

14

"Stand by your word." (8. ii)

The Chinese ideogram for honor
is a human beside an open mouth:
standing by one's word. One

of the riddles of the Sphinx was:
What do you give to another,
and still must keep?

Your word.
The fool promises at night, and
in the morning has forgotten;

he agrees too readily, thus
his word is not trusted.
The wise are reluctant to promise,

thoughtful and slow to give their word,
but once given,
they will move heaven and Earth

to stand by their word.

15

"Sharpen a blade too much and its edge is lost." (9)

The fool goes on grinding
long after the blade of the sword
has found its balance, thus

the blade does not make a clean cut
and the blood goes everywhere, stains the carpet.
The wise sharpen the blade

until the edge is fine enough
to split the length of a single hair
and then they stop,

apply a fine coat
of the most precious oil,
and with one thrust

they pierce the heart.
When they withdraw,
one drop of blood is on the tip:

this is called Death By A Timely Word.

16

"In the opening and shutting of heaven's gate, can you play the feminine part?" (10)

The fool is aggressive, uses force
and coercion, violence and fear
to achieve his ends: he scorns

and seeks to dominate the Feminine;
this is fear distorting the Masculine.
Heaven's gate is the present; it opens

when the wise use the Masculine
to hold attention lower down in the body,
moving neither towards, nor away from,

the lure of desire. This allows the Feminine
to emerge in safety to receive, remaining
open and vulnerable, impregnated with

Consciousness. The Masculine remains
vigilant, actively-passive, creating sanctuary,
serving the Feminine which gives birth

to Non-Judgmental Love.

17

"The chase and the hunt craze people's minds." (12)

The fool prefers to remain
a complicated little status-quo machine
fueled by his personal history

and enslaved
by unconscious inner forces
over which he has no control.

It is these forces which create
the chase and the hunt:
we chase after what we already have

and hunt for what lies hidden within;
but when the mind releases its grip
through careful and unceasing vigilance,

because it cannot stand to be seen
in the clear light of scrutiny,
the immeasurable Stillness stands revealed:

poised, elegant, voluptuous in Its praise of emptiness.

18

"Favor and disgrace seem alarming." (13)

Those who do not have favor
seek it, and will tie themselves
into whatever knot pleases;

once they have found favor
they fear losing it and
will assume any posture

to keep it;
they fear disgrace will cause them
to lose it.

The fool looks for favor
in the wrong places, whereas
the wise know that all favor lies

in the present, the now-of-the-body;
they stay close to the body and
recover their senses: nothing to gain,

therefore, nothing to lose.

19

**"Stay with the ancient Tao,
move with the present."** (14) (Gia-Fu Feng)

The destination is the present;
it must be constantly renewed
with every breath, otherwise

the connection is lost.
The present is the Ancient-Mother,
the source of all creation,

infinite and immortal. The fool
searches endlessly for the door
to freedom; the doorway to the present

remains always wide open and inviting
if one travels barefoot, down into the body,
but the fool's attention is snared, taken

by the shadows which thought throws
upon the cave wall of the mind. Believing
in his thoughts, the fool remains forever

enslaved by shadows, dazzled by darkness.

20

"[The ancient masters were] alert, like one aware of danger."
(15) (Gia-Fu Feng)

The thief awaits the smallest opening
to enter the house and
steal what is precious there.

So the wise remain vigilant;
when the merest shadow
darkens the window,

momentarily blocking the light,
they return to the Mother, who is
always and only present:

Her protection never fails.
The mind acting alone is dangerous,
moving from fascination to fascination,

oblivious to the consequences.
Stay close to the Mother, and mind
faithfully serves Her grace, reflecting

the light of Her mercy.

21

"He who keeps the Tao…does not rush to early ripening."
(15. ii)

The young slattern whose body ripens
before her emotions mature, opens
to any stranger and is young

no longer; camp-fondled and badly used,
she too-soon loses her bloom, her Soul is
bruised and her looks decay; she's quick

to blame her troubles on her circumstance,
on bad fortune, luck or chance,
but never on her own ignorance.

The wise poet is in no rush to please the crowd,
suspects the poem of which he's overly proud,
and will not read his rough drafts aloud;

instead he works patiently at revision;
he knows that going slow is the best decision.
The wise bloom only in their season

and do not rush the plant for any reason.

22

**"[The ancient masters are] watchful, like men crossing a
winter stream.** (15. iii) (Gia-Fu Feng)

The Way is narrow and easily lost,
no matter how far along the path you've traveled;
the loss of vigilance has a dear cost,

the thread of wisdom is easily unraveled.
It is a wise man who watches his thought,
pays close attention to his emotion,

and knows the inner world is fraught
with danger. He is like one on a raft in the ocean,
always studying the horizon for the coming storm.

A man crossing a winter stream
listens for the subtlest crack
and never goes so far in he can't turn back.

If you chain the leg of a baby elephant to a stake,
when he is grown you may bind him with a thread
and he will remain forever bound. He is like a man

who does not watch his thoughts.

23

**"To fulfill one's destiny is to be constant...
Knowing the constant gives perspective."** (16)

The constant lover looks neither
to the right nor to the left, but
is focused always on the Beloved;

even when he is on the meditation cushion
and his mind is still, his heart
sneaks out of the room to be with the Beloved.

This constancy allows the watcher to see
how the emotions swirl over every pretty face,
and the shapely thigh causes the mind to race;

his is the perspective of the still boulder
in the middle of the racing stream.
Fate is governed by chance and by the dream,

but destiny is not under the Law of Accident;
when the attention is constant,
the help that comes is provident

and one's true destiny becomes evident.

24

"The greatest leader…leaves no trace." (17)

She is called the Hidden Yogi, the one
who has mastered herself and works,
not on the Ashram or upon a throne,

but in the soup kitchen, alone
among the bustling crowd;
her Dharma is never loud,

calls no attention to herself,
yet the kitchen help is drawn to her
and the Dharma comes through her

cooking and her handling of dispute
when trouble arises at the stove or sink;
her touch is so gentle that the people think

it is they who've solved the problem.
Her Presence brings a smile to every face
and when at last she leaves, there is no trace

of her going, but the kitchen is a better place.

25

"Give up sainthood, renounce wisdom." (19)

The fool acts wise, behaves
in a way he thinks a saint behaves,
and all the while he is looking

to be worshipped, to be loved, looking
for anything to cover the absence
of self-worth. However,

the wise man knows he is no saint,
would blush and turn away if
anyone called him saint, even

his own Master; if anyone should bow
to him, he returns the bow, knowing
the saintliness of all sentient Beings;

he knows that wisdom does not come from him,
but is a gift given freely to all who
live in the present: fertile soil yields abundance,

no matter who plants the seed.

26

"No mind, no worries." (20)

Maybe you have seen this picture
of the Good Master Jesus which shows His
Heart in flames in the middle of His chest,

a crown of thorns encircling it,
and a bright light emanating from it,
while his head is encircled by a softer,

reflected light which we call a halo.
Just as the Moon gives off no light of its own,
but reflects the light from Our Sun,

in exactly this same way, the mind
gives no light, but reflects the light
from the awakened heart. Self remembering

burns off the impurities of the heart,
self observation the impurities of the mind;
the still mind faithfully serves

as the heart kindly rules.

27

"What is the difference between 'yes' and 'no'?" (20. ii)

Desire is the endless chase
between "yes" and "no."
One chases after desire

the way a stray dog
chases after the meat wagon,
hoping a scrap will fall in the dust

and when one should chance to do so,
it is vicious in its efforts
to ward off all interlopers

as it swallows without chewing,
devours without tasting. The path of desire
has no end, thus it offers no satisfaction.

Seeing this, one may rest in the Stillness.
Absent desire, fear ceases and
the Mother opens Her arms;

the dog lies down at Her feet.

28

**"Mine is indeed the mind of an ignoramus
in its unadulterated simplicity...
Indeed I seem like an idiot."** (20. iii)

If I tell you my secret you will stone me:
I am an Idiot. People ask me to go
here and there, to speak and to teach,

so I go with nothing to say,
not knowing how it will go and
I stand before them like a gray cloud

on an overcast day, waiting for the Light
to break through. And when It does,
as It always does, I appear

brilliant and people applaud. But
I tell you I am as the Moon whose
brilliance is a reflection of the Sun.

People do not want to see that I am
just another Idiot in the street whom the dogs
come to, seeking scraps: they know I have

a few crumbs in my pocket from the King's table.

29

"The greatest virtue is to follow the Tao and the Tao alone."
(21)

The fool wanders the alleys of the town,
moving from tavern to tavern
seeking that drunkenness which will

take him from the cares of the world;
he lays with every bar whore,
cunt-stunned and flesh-whipped,

stinking of the sweet perfumes, tongue
flapping like a torn flag on the battlements.
The wise are single-minded like a good dog

laying at the feet of the Master,
taking what is placed in his bowl,
drunk from the scent of the Beloved;

having no more cares, they follow the Law
and remain in the Tavern of Ruin
where the laughter scandalizes the town

and they are undone, ravished, annihilated in love.

30

"Fierce winds do not blow all day." (23)

The Way is straight and narrow, it is
difficult and will trouble a man's sleep
until he gains his center of gravity;

self observation will strip all his buffers
and he will see himself as he is, not
as he pretends to be, not as he wishes to be,

but exactly as he is; thus
he suffers, and he suffers exceedingly
the more he observes. That is why the fool

yields to the urge to run from self-knowledge,
because it shatters his dreams;
he sells his Soul to the devil. But

the wise know that such suffering builds endurance,
will not last forever, thus they bear their urges
with faith, tolerance, and perseverance

until sky clears, winds cease, and Sun emerges.

PLATE 1   **Doris Kreickhaus, artist**

Trailing Flowers and Fish
The softest thing in the universe overcomes the hardest thing in the universe. Watercolor on rice paper. 27.25 in. h x 13.5 in. w

PLATE 2   **Doris Kreickhaus, artis**

Migrating Birds
Something mysteriously formed, before heaven and earth. Watercolor or
rice paper. 16.75 in. h x 25.25 in. w

Untitled

A concise and metaphorical expression of the birth, travel and return of
the soul to the origin, the Mother, and the whole created in the union of
the opposites. Colored ink on cardboard. 8.46 in. h x 5.5 in. w

PLATE 4   Michelle Meaux, artist

Side 2

She is fanâ'—the disappearance of self into the blessing sound of the Universe.
Her total receptivity transforms her into an embodiment of adoration at the
feet of the Mother. Oil on wood engraving, 21 in. h x 12 in. w

PLATE 5

Still Life

Form comes into being from the earth Mother, fulfills a function: Life. When that function ends, Form returns to Her. Acrylic on canvas. 20 in. w x 16 in. h

PLATE 6

Crowning Glory

The flower is the reproductive organ of the plant. We spring from the earth Mother and as winter follows fall, we return to Her. Acrylic on canvas. 26 in. w x 36 in. h

PLATE 7

Kuan Yin

This is the face of serenity and understanding, invoking the ultimate compassion of the Mother. This sculptural wall mask combines ceramics, paint and imbedded beads. 9.5 in. w x 14.5 in. h

PLATE 8

Sleeping Woman

She represents the healing and nurturing nature of Mother Earth, with her hair of leaves and dewdrops of pearls. This sculptural wall mask combines ceramics, glaze and imbedded beads. 11.5 in. w x 13.5 in. h

PLATE 9   **Jocelyn del Rio, artist**

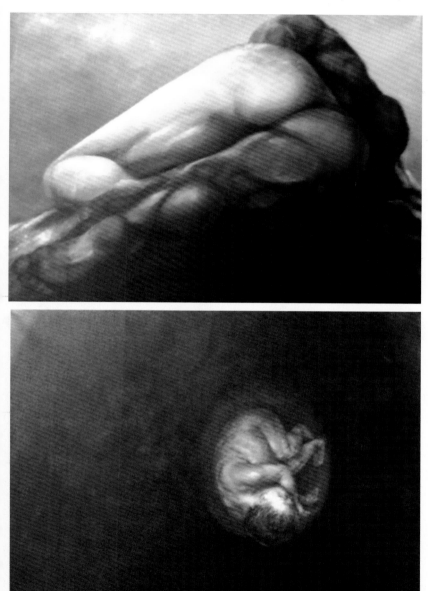

Ixtlaccihuatl

An Aztec princess falls into a bewitched sleep and in her stillness becomes part of a volcanic range. Those who believe in her, over the centuries, long for her revival, for the fulfillment of her possibility, of the seed within her giving birth to a new culture. Diptych—acrylic on primed cotton. 2 ft. 5 in. w x 3 ft. 8 in. h

PLATE 10   Jocelyn del Rio, artist

The Sleeping Woman Must Give Birth
Ixtlaccihuatl lies as still as a mountain, breathing as the earth itself breathes
Her love on guard beside her, keeping both alive with inner volcanic
activity. They await the birth that is foreseen and longed for by many. Oil
on primed cotton, hung as a diamond. 3 ft. 4 in. square

PLATE 11

Jocelyn del Rio, artist

Cihuateteo

This is the name given to women who die in childbirth. The Aztecs honored them as warriors for their dying to save life. They were buried on shields, with the adornments of true warriorship and destined to be reborn as sacred hummingbirds. Oil on a wooden cable spool. 4 ft. diameter

PLATE 12   Jocelyn del Rio, artist

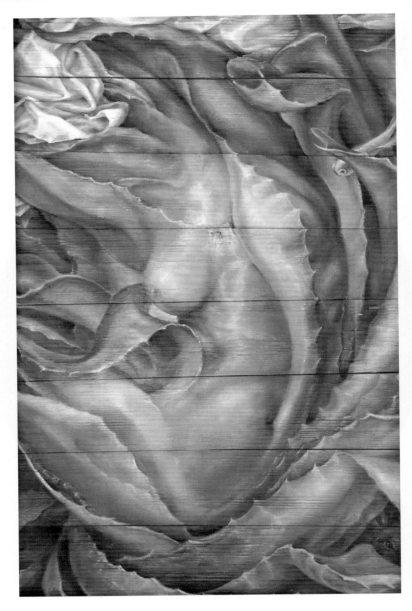

Mayahuel

Mayahuel ran away with her divine lover and fell from the tree where she
hid. Her body broke into many pieces, duly buried, which sprouted into
agave plants. Her relationship to the Divine became manifest in reliable
evolving gifts to humanity, symbolized by the fish which comes to suckle
at her breast. Oil on native split pine. 3 ft. 5 in. h x 2 ft. 5 in. w

31

**"There was something formless and perfect
before the universe was born…
It is the Mother of the universe." (25)**

The present is without form or name.
I know, I know: calling it the present,
the here-now, is the past

naming a concept, like
a drunken sailor yelling at the wind
to cease so he can get his bearings.

The present, the Mother, the Tao
cannot be named because it is not
congruent with the past; they exist

in different dimensions. This naming is
dangerous; it seems to explain the Mother.
To be held by the Mother is not the same

as speaking of Her, in the same way
that saying the word "fire" is not the same
as being warmed by a fire.

Thus…

32

"To know the Way, understand the great within yourself."
(25. ii)

A hen cannot give birth to a dog,
nor can a stone placed in the soil
produce a tree.

Each thing births that which is
in its own image, like itself and
of its own nature.

We come from Greatness and
we return from whence we came.
Greatness can only birth Greatness,

this is the Law.
The mind cannot comprehend Greatness
because it is a recoil into fear, a strategy

to avoid Greatness. Fear
is the absence of Greatness; mind
is blind to all but its own contents, thus

remember yourself and know Greatness.

33

**"If you let yourself be blown to and fro,
you lose touch with your root."** (26)

Down low in the body is the root
which anchors plant and holds the soil intact,
so wind does not blow all your soil away

and creeping vine survives to bear its fruit.
When mind alone rules, everything distracts
attention from the present; we betray

our nature like lambs at lambing time
sold to the butcher. Once you've lost touch
with your root, any breeze blows you off your course,

and then there is no wickedness or crime
too heinous, unthinkable, or out of reach;
you veer from here to there like a horse

who's lost its rider, dumbstruck and alone.
The wise always stay close to the root-bone,
down where they feel the Soul when it weeps

and where attention lives and never sleeps.

34

"Truly the best governor governs least." (28)

It is a truly strong man
who governs from Stillness
and does not interfere.

It is a wise mother who
protects her child from real harm, but
allows him scrapes and bruises and

to make his own mistakes;
it is by trial and error that a good dog
learns to leave the hen house out of reach

before he gets shot. The child who's allowed
to follow her own nature wherever it leads
will grow in self-worth, not following the crowd

but practicing kindness:
whoever rules with kindness
never needs to use force; the people serve

gladly, from love of kindness.

35

"Trying to grasp, we lose." (29)

The fool chases after happiness
like a dog after its own tail;
thus, it remains always out of reach.

It is the same with love:
it does not come from us, but
to us from Our Creator, so

trying to hold onto it,
seeking to control it, is like
the man with a teaspoon

trying to hold back the river.
The wise do not try to find love, but
remain always relaxed

and in the present
where love can find them; those who
give drink and expect none in return

find their cup overflowing.

36

"Trying to control leads to ruin." (29. ii)

The fool who tries to control love
is like the man with a spoon
trying to empty the ocean and

cursing the incoming tide.
We are little and love is great: it comes
as Grace to us if we do not interfere;

it does not judge, only forgives;
fear refuses to forgive because
it does not trust love.

Love is a blessing-force for all creation.
What ruins love is seeking to control
what is Divine, a force from another dimension.

Among the wise, love is in control and
they bow down and serve. Fear drives men mad,
it is the absence of love. Fear separates.

Love unites.

37

"After a great battle...the earth lies stripped of its Motherhood...You must never think of conquering others by force." (30)

Where the Mother Spirit rules,
peace prevails. It is the same among families
as among nations: when a family is governed

by the Mother Spirit, both parents are held
and they in turn hold their children;
they do not harm the children physically,

verbally, or emotionally; they resolve conflict
without violence, using gentleness and calm
where others rule by force; the hand which

strokes the child's face
does not strike the child's body. The Mother Spirit
is kind and all feel safe where She prevails.

The child who is not hit has great self-worth,
the child who is held has dignity and courage,
the child disciplined by reason is reasonable:

fear rules by force, Motherhood by kindness.

38

"Arms serve evil." (31)

Fear rules by force of arms and
believes evil can be held at bay
by violence; to trust love

is inconceivable to fear because
it exists only in love's absence;
violence begins with a single thought:

a single drop of fear
contaminates a hundred rivers and
the water is no longer fit to drink.

Where the people are heavily armed,
terror is their natural state; arms
always produce more arms, there is

no end to it until the land is barren,
the children curse their birth, and
the women turn away from the men in fear:

violence begets evil, as far as the heart can see.

"Know when to stop." (32)

I've known men hard as nails
who left bruises and called it love
and they'd drink until they drop,

but rarest of all among men
is one who knows when to stop.
Most men lack real self control,

they couldn't care less at the toll
that violence exacts on their Soul
and I'd put my Father at the top,

but most precious of all among men
is one who knows when to stop.
I was raised by a man with a cruel streak

so I came by one as the seed of his crop;
by many men I was justly reviled,
but when I raised a harsh hand to my child,

that's how I learned when to stop.

40

**"Conquering others requires force.
Conquering yourself takes power."** (33) (Hamill)

What profits a man if he makes great art
and has not mastered himself?
If every wayward thought commands his heart

he is a mere trinket on a pauper's shelf.
What matter if the world bows down before him
if he is not lord of his own emotions;

he is a slave though the world adore him,
a beggar though he rules the oceans.
The man who is master of his moods,

he alone is able to stand by his word;
his face belongs to him, not to his attitudes.
Though many admire him, he is a solitary bird

who flies always to the highest peak.
He keeps his own counsel, when all about him speak.
There is no suffering like self observation,

no joy like its slow and subtle transformation.

41

**"Conquering others requires force.
Conquering yourself takes power."** (33. ii) (Hamill)

The fool confuses fear
with respect; likewise
he confuses force

with power. If the trap
of clarity is using it
to try to change others,

rather than seeing oneself clearly,
then the trap of power is
using it to control others,

rather than mastering oneself.
Power over others is tyranny;
power over one's habits and functions

is enlightenment, not attained by force,
but by vigilance and forgiveness.
Forgiveness is the power

no force can overwhelm.

42

"The gentle outlasts the strong." (36)

Just as the wind, which can be seen
only by its effect on other things,
wears tall mountain down

grain by grain,
so too water
which is soft and yielding,

like the Feminine,
wears a hole through the stone
drop by drop.

In this same way
love overcomes fear.
Not by force

but by gentle persuasion,
patience and loving kindness,
the wild dog is made to lie down

and lick the proffered hand.

43

"The gentle outlasts the strong." (36. ii)

One of the riddles of the Sphinx was:
What moves among men unseen,
kills the strongest without violence,

and levels empires?
Time is the great leveler,
the implacable foe.

In this same way, I was a cold,
frightened, angry and insensitive man,
selfish, blind to the feelings of others.

Then my wife made her entrance into my life;
where once Saturday night romance
was my only dance, her loving kindness,

just her gentle glance, worked
its magic in my cold and broken heart,
opening it to adoration,

preparing it for love's annihilation.

44

"The wise do nothing, yet nothing is left undone." (37)

Just across the pond
from where I am sitting,
an old Turtle rests on a tree

which has fallen into the water;
he is awash in Sunlight, neck
outstretched toward the Sun

in prayerful repose.
He is doing nothing and
everything is taken care of,

wants nothing and
everything is given to him,
takes no thought

for tomorrow nor
is he troubled
by the concerns of the day:

a true practitioner of the Way.

45

"The highest kindness is to give without condition." (38)

The fool is cunning, always
looking for opportunity,
seeking an advantage,

dealing from the bottom of the deck;
he gives to seek favor,
to win position, and

because he covets the return.
The awakened heart considers
only the other, never the self;

the wise give because their cup is overflowing
and all about them thirst, thus
they withhold nothing because

the well never runs dry.
He who has one blanket and
gives it to him who has none

will never want for a place by the stove.

46

"Ritual is the husk of true faith." (38. ii)

The mind insists on ritual
when the Spirit
has fled the form;

it clings to belief
when there is no direct experience;
ritual is fear

clothed in the robes of sanctity;
it is the substitute for faith.
True faith is not belief, but

arises from the direct experience
of the Divine in action;
it is born from questioning

and doubt, from refusal
to take the word of another.
True faith comes when the fool's heart

is overwhelmed by grace and mercy.

"The great master follows his own nature." (38. iii)
(For Alec Wilkinson. *The New Yorker*, 9/09/2013.)

The Great White Shark
is a killing machine.
Its underside is white and

its top is gray so it is sometimes called
the man in a gray suit.
It is by nature solitary,

so does not travel in a school
like other fish. It swims
and eats; that is its nature.

It is single-minded, slow and deliberate
in the hunt; it owns the ocean and
it lives strictly on its own terms.

Like the great Master it is Impersonal.
Life makes one promise: you will die;
once you are in the ocean,

you are simply part of the food chain.

48

"Yielding is the way of the Tao." (40)

The wise contend with no one
for they are content with nothing,
therefore they have everything, so

what is there to fight over?
They neither argue nor debate
because a single word

thoughtfully spoken
satisfies the need and
fulfills what is necessary.

The more words,
the greater the misunderstanding.
The wise dwell in Stillness,

emptiness is their nature,
solitude is their constant companion.
When the wise are challenged, they

yield and bow with folded hands.

49

"The easy way seems hard." (41)

Before the Way is made easy,
the mind will make it hard;
it will throw up countless obstacles

which it then labors like a man on fire
to overcome; it will cast doubt
upon troubled waters like a foolish man

casting dynamite into the stream, then
collecting the dead fish and
boasting in the village about his catch.

Yet patient observation reveals that
all difficulties arise in the mind,
are self-made from the personal history,

like placing a straw man on a stick, then
fleeing in terror from it in the dark.
The easy Way is when the Mother is allowed

to do Her Work without interference.

50

"The greatest art seems unsophisticated." (41. ii)

In art, as in life, simpler
is better: telling the truth in plain language,
directness, absence of style,

wisdom in the small detail,
leaving the tool marks
on wood or marble,

are often frowned upon
for their simplicity and
apparent lack of sophistication.

But the greatest art is the emergence
in the ordinary man of humility and reticence,
the simple truth, the refusal

to dress up the body or the teaching
to appeal to fashion or good taste;
real taste is love of beauty and

real beauty is honest heart.

51

"The greatest love seems indifferent." (41. iii)

The greatest love is Holy, and
wholly impartial, which does not mean
cold, uncaring; it means

without judgment, indifferent
regarding the arising of phenomena;
it loves all equally, beggar

and saint, friend and enemy.
The fool says he is "in love"
which is how fear distorts relationship:

the mind seeks an object to focus on;
it seeks to claim and control, and
it calls this love.

The greatest love is without preference,
Emptiness showering its fullness:
the Sun warms flower and beast alike,

shines its light upon the darkest heart.

52

"The greatest wisdom seems childish." (41. iv)

The child is innocent by nature,
not by choice, thus
the world steals this treasure from her

because she has not paid for it;
first we lose,
then we may choose. But

the road back is difficult, straight
and narrow is the Way and it is
filled with traps and obstacles;

those who prevail are said to be
"*like* little children," Jesus said,
but they are *not* little children, because

theirs is a wise-innocence;
their wisdom is simple, *like* a child's;
they delight in play, *like* a child, but

they choose innocence, and they know the price.

53

"One gains by losing." (42)

Self importance is like a hot dry wind
which raises a great cloud of dust but
robs the soil of its nutrients.

Observing it without judgment,
grain by grain it is diminished and
slowly, slowly what stands revealed

is what lay concealed beneath the dust cloud:
the Being feeds from self importance
the way the chick in the eggshell

feeds from the yolk until
it has gathered strength to break through.
In that same way

the Being emerges as self importance diminishes;
the Feminine gains ascendance
as the Masculine yields:

the Mother emerges from Her solitude.

54

**"That without substance can enter where there is no room.
Hence I know the value of non-action."** (43) (Gia-Fu Feng)

One of the riddles of the Sphinx was:
"What has no substance, yet
can defeat all that is substantial?"

Attention has no substance, yet
it burns everything in its path until
it alone remains: when this occurs

it is called "Silent Witness."
Everything which has substance becomes
non-substantial: all forms die.

Emptiness remains. The mind and its doing
leave no room within. Doing nothing, not
interfering, the Witness empties the crowded room

so the Will-of-Our-Creator may act.
That without substance
enters the broken heart, where once

there was no room for it in the Inn.

55

"Love is the fruit of sacrifice." (44)

When it is mature, love
considers others before itself.
My love has flown west.

Like a lone bird
winging its way
into the fading light,

she has gone to nurse
our dying friend
in what remains of daylight.

This is what she's always done,
carried her love like an oil lamp
into the shadow of death,

holding the dying in her arms,
her love a steady beacon
by which the Soul may orient itself

as it wings its ancient way heavenward.

56

"Love is the fruit of sacrifice." (44. ii)

She had the most beautiful brown eyes I have
ever seen, like deep pools of sweet Maple syrup.
One time I came into a room and she came through

the other door and we moved to one another like twins
joined at the heart: she began to speak but I was
lost, drowning, gone, hopelessly gone in those eyes

and then in mid-sentence she
stopped and took off her glasses and
she looked so deeply into me that we both

began to laugh like little children and this was
the kind of laughter which is honest and real and
tears the heart out; then she put her head against mine

and we loved one another, in that moment, forever.
We were both married, so it went no further. Now,
when I feel her, I do not go there; some things are

so precious that you have to leave them alone.

57

"What you gain is more trouble than what you lose." (44. iii)

The scholar fills himself with knowledge
but remains a fool because
he believes he knows something;

the build-up of silt
causes the dam to break;
the accumulation of riches

attracts thieves.
There is no end to gaining,
no amount can displace fear.

The wise give away their riches
as fast as they receive them, thus
they remain beggars, always

walking with an empty bowl,
still mind, nothing left
to lose: who can steal their Wisdom

when they give it freely to every passing stranger?

"Great intelligence seems stupid." (45)

When Mister Lee brought students to Him,
the Mad Beggar Yogi Ramsuratkumar wept.
"This Beggar has nothing to teach you,"

He cried. All knowledge had fled,
the knower had died, left
only an empty bowl where the head

once overflowed.
The greater the intelligence,
the simpler the form,

the fewer the words to convey it.
Yogi Ramsuratkumar once lived on the street,
begged in the town for something to eat,

and the bad boys often beat Him;
they thought Him a witless fool.
He only forgave them, remained a still pool

with the Moon reflected in it.

59

"When the world has the Way…
warhorses…till the fields." (46)

In the ancient teachings
the emotions were likened to a horse, and
it was said that in the fool

this horse had thrown its rider
and ran rough-shod over the field
like a warhorse terrified

of the gunfire, yellow teeth bared,
the whites of its eyes rolled back.
Now take this horse and feed it the hay

of self-restraint gathered on the Way;
it is not broken by force, but tamed
by attention and the grace of the unnamed

and unnamable Presence awakened within:
he may race over field and hollow
but will gracefully yield to pull the plow;

lead him by gentleness alone, and he will follow.

"Contentment alone is enough." (46. ii)

The fool is driven by his doing,
waving a stick in front of him
and jabbering the air, spittle

flying like soot from a broken chimney,
flailing the stick first this way
then that, stopping dead-stride

and looking around for praise,
holding the stick aloft like Caesar
entering the city triumphant.

He lives for the accolade, while
the wise remain invisible and Still.
Resting in the present, obeying the Law,

contentment arises
like the water in the spring
following a storm; it does not seek,

neither does it reject what is given.

61

"The farther one goes, the less one knows." (47)

Zen has called the journey to the present
"the journey of a single step," and
that is the journey of attention and presence

down into the body, to the root. It is
a long and difficult journey from
the mind and its fear,

to the body and its presence: the body
exists in one way as an objective-
feedback-instrument to orient the Being

in the present, thus locating the Being
in the presence of the Mother. Once
one enters Her domain, all knowing, all

personal history, all knowledge is left
for the Lord of Death to consume. Naked and
vulnerable, safe and protected in the Mother,

we wander in wise ignorance into the Mystery.

62

"True mastery can be gained by letting things go their own way." (48)

The fool thrives on interference,
gives advice when none is asked for and
cannot leave well enough alone. Thus

he is twice a fool:
once for believing he must speak and
once for speaking.

He refuses
to allow others to learn
from their own mistakes.

The wise allow the water to take
its own course downhill and seek
its own level. They hold their tongues

and allow others to find their way
through trial and error, just as
they themselves stumbled upon wisdom

through a field strewn with broken dreams.

63

"[The Sage] dwells in that place where death cannot enter."
(50)

The Sacred Heart of Mercy arises
from brokenness;
it is not given to the fearful,

but to those with strength to grow meek
beneath the force of a broken heart,
which means they find courage to surrender

to the suffering without show
or complaint,
they endure the suffering of the Saint

who carried His own Cross up the hill
and they are transformed by Divine Will
into an impossible gentleness: the stone

is rolled away and they are allowed
to enter into the Sacred Heart of Mercy
where Death has no dominion, a safe place

when the forest is burning.

64

**"All things arise from the Tao.
They are nourished by virtue."** (51) (Gia-Fu Feng)

Mothers, fathers, daughters, sons, what
is the source of real beauty if not virtue, and
what is virtue if not love of the Mother

shining forth from within
the Sacred Heart of Mercy? Real beauty
is not the slave of time, therefore

it is untouched by the Angel of Doom;
it never fades, but feeds that love
which passes all understanding.

In the absence of virtue, fear reigns supreme,
casting its dismal shadow darkly
across the barren fields, thus

the crops fail, they do not yield
nourishment and the people starve.
Where there is virtue, the harvest

is abundant and the granaries overflow.

65

**"He who is filled with Virtue is like a newborn child.
Wasps and serpents will not sting him.** (55) (Gia-Fu Feng)

The fewer the laws,
the greater a nation's virtue.
The loss of a nation's virtue

is marked by the abundance of laws
and of patriots, each vying
with the other to show off

his righteousness; the arguments
for violating the Laws of Decency
are always glib and honey-tongued

but they cannot hide the viper's fang,
nor dilute its venom.
Once a nation has lost its virtue

it will find enemies on all sides, and
despite its force of arms
it will be brought down

by a boy with a slingshot.

66

"Close your mouth." (56)

The mouth is the gateway:
what goes in will not befoul a man
half so much as what comes out,

Jesus said. By closing the gate
one listens more and
every living thing begins to speak

in tongues unknown to the mind.
When a fool opens the gate
a torrent rushes forth and

there is no end to the trouble;
the village is torn with strife,
husband is set against wife,

and scandal plagues the heart.
The Sufis say to open the gate only
when what one has to say

is greater than the Silence.

67

"Guard the senses. (56. ii)

The fool allows the senses free reign.
Thus, they are like a horse
who runs rough-shod over the terrain,

leaving chaos and pain
everywhere in its wake and
burning through its promise

before it has a chance to gain
maturity. The wise keep close watch
on the senses, husband their force

like a cistern holds the rain,
so there is plenty of good water
even in the dry season.

When the senses are restrained,
good sense arises and
attention guards the gate, so

only loving kindness may enter.

68

"The more advanced the weapons of state, the darker the nation." (57)

Oh twisted fool in your hovel of ruin,
how you bend in dim light
over your engineer's schematics

for the doomsday weapon which will
give you the level of power
which your level of fear demands:

bloody is the wasted plain,
brick-strewn the cityscape,
torn, broken, limb-lost and

riven are the bodies stacked
like cordwood. Meanwhile,
the wise are armed only with the Law,

not its letter, but its spirit,
felicitous of the form, but never slavish to it;
they alone are secure, fear no evil, live

free from the shadow of Death.

69

"[The Master] illuminates but does not dazzle." (58)

The scholar dazzles with his brilliance,
leaving his audience feeling foolish
in their ignorance;

he is a liar without knowing it, because
his mind is full of borrowed knowledge
which he passes off as if it were

his own experience. He is
a collector of books,
not of experience.

He will defeat the wise in argument
every time, because once they speak the Truth
they will fall silent, while he cites

passage after passage to disprove.
The wise will not blind with a spotlight
when a candle will do

to illuminate a darkened room.

"Nothing surpasses thrift and moderation." (59)

The fool lives a life of dreadful waste, squanders
the beauty of the Earth, spoils its gift
by the way he pillages and plunders,

but the wise live a simple life of thrift;
they leave every place they live
better than they found it, and their only

wish is not what they can get, but what give
back so they do not die from a lonely
Spirit sucked dry by greed.

He who lives a simple, thrifty life
takes from the Earth only what he needs,
no more. Just as he would never harm his wife,

it would break his heart to harm the earth;
in good husbandry, the Soul finds its worth.
Thrift and moderation have great utility,

and give rise to a thoughtful humility.

"The female overcomes the male with stillness." (61)

It is the Masculine which moves attention
out of the mind, down into the body
where the Feminine waits for the sign

that it is safe to emerge;
that sign is the presence of attention
in Her dwelling place, in the present.

She is Stillness, and it is this quality
which overwhelms the Masculine force
and gives rise to devotion.

Her Stillness draws Him back,
over and over; She builds Her nest
of Stillness, Her Love is Stillness; thus

the Masculine becomes passive, as devotion, and
the Feminine becomes active, as love. This is
the perfect union: love and devotion

from which adoration is born.

72

**"The Tao is the treasure-house, the true nature,
the secret source of everything."** (62)

Self observation is like water dripping
to wear away stone: yes, it reveals
all of the impurities, the hypocrisies,

the contradictions, the excuses and
the excesses; it requires
the greatest courage and

even greater patience to endure
what the slow, steady drip exposes.
But as the patient prospector

washes and washes through her screen,
slowly the dirt, the effluvia are washed away
and pure gold, shining Goodness,

the great kindness is revealed
beneath the outer coating: it is a gradual
wearing-away so all that remains is

one's true nature: Non-Judgmental Love.

73

"Achieve greatness in little things." (63)

God is in the details, Mies van der Rohe said,
and by this he meant give careful attention
to what is right in front of you,

be watchful of the step you are taking
now, and
do not get too far ahead of yourself;

by remaining with attention
always in the present,
God will find you.

The mind strays far afield,
yearning always for tomorrow;
thus, the fool lives in sorrow, but

the wise seek to master little things,
find joy in precision;
he who takes care of the little things

never gets into big trouble.

74

"The Sage does not act, and so is not defeated." (64) (Gia-Fu Feng)

The mind reacts to the first impulse of thought
and therefore enters the world of trouble;
the emotions react to the first impulse of survival

and therefore enter the world of problems.
What is the difference between action and
non-action, between doing and not-doing?

The wise respond to the first faint stirring
of Conscience,
such a still small feeling like the breath

of a bird stirring the stillness of air; this
response is called the "Effortless-Effort," and
it occurs before thought makes trouble, before

emotion makes a problem. Conscience is truth,
and truth can never be defeated; to respond
when Conscience stirs is called "non-action"

because it is not my will, but Thine.

75

"The simplest pattern is the clearest." (65)

The mind thrives on complexity, conflict
and confusion, cannot tolerate
simplicity because

then it has nothing to do,
nothing to worry about,
what is simple becomes clear.

With simplicity, the troubled waters
grow quiet, the muddy pond
settles and

the water becomes sweet and clear.
The simple man sharpens his tools:
presence and attention;

he cares for them the way the good farmer
cares for the land, as precious as his family;
by working deeply in the soil of the heart

weeds disappear. Love blooms.

76

"Humility is power. (66)

The fool seeks power in force,
asserts his will over others
by violence of the body or

of the Spirit,
does not govern his thoughts,
does harm in word and deed;

he rules by fear, believing
this is the way to gain respect.
It is a wise one who listens

when all around him speak,
leads by following the Law
of Heaven, corrects

by gentle means, is humbled
by love and when kindness
does not work,

he tries more kindness.

**"I have three treasures which I hold fast
and watch closely…"** (67)

i. The first is mercy.

Forgiveness is the greatest mercy, thus
it comes with the greatest price:
surrender of the desire for revenge;

if kindness is the greatest virtue,
mercy is the greatest kindness.
The fool rejects mercy, because

it appears to be weakness among men,
thus he seeks to pluck out the eye
of the enemy who has taken his eye;

because he believes mercy comes from
him alone, and alone he cannot grant it,
he acts without mercy.

Mercy comes from Above, thus
the Masculine holds firmly in place, and
the Feminine receives grace; together

they serve the Sacred Heart of Mercy.

"I have three treasures…" (67)

ii. The second is frugality.

The fool squanders his inner force
in identification with thought,
obeying every vagrant emotion, and

surrendering to every mood, thus
he lives under the Law of Accident
and is wasted by old age.

The wise are frugal with experience,
husbanding its force by taking no position
regarding the arising of phenomena,

neither for nor against.
Thus they prolong their life; they do not
spend the precious coins in their purse

on baubles, mere trinkets, and
sounding brass; they invest all their wealth
in Conscience, thus they live

in abundance, all the days of their life.

"I have three treasures…" (67)

iii. The third is humility.

There are 4 great traps on the Way.
The first is fear: the fool boasts
and swaggers, attacks without mercy

in order to cover up his fear; the wise
return to the Mother, who comforts and
protects from all fear, thus they are humbled.

The second is clarity: the fool uses it
to try to change others, constantly interfering;
the wise use it to observe themselves, thus

they are humbled.
The third is power; the fool uses it
to rule others, but the wise to rule themselves,

thus they are humbled. The last
is old age; the fool weakened by excess, collapses;
the wise follow the Way gratefully to the end, humbled

because grace and mercy give them love of the Way.

80

"A good fighter is not angry." (68)

Make no mistake about it, when one
undertakes the practice of self remembering,
the battle is joined, the fight is on and

something must die. But,
it is not like you think, this fight:
when there is a reaction of any kind

to what is observed, either anger or joy,
the battle is already lost; this is called
identification and what is created is

a stone dropped into a still pool
disrupting the calm surface, an anomaly
in the electrical field which is the body.

The fight is never against, but for more presence,
always struggling to remain present, here-now,
no anger, no judgment, no reaction:

no fight, no blame.

81

**"There is no greater misfortune
than feeling 'I have an enemy.'"** (69)

The trap of self observation is seeing
what is observed as an enemy
to be attacked and conquered; thus,

"myself" is constantly carried from the field
on its shield, bloodied and beaten,
defeated. The "yes" is an energetic entity

against which the "no" can push,
a Lawful opposing force which creates friction,
without which there can be no movement.

The present is the unknown, a presence
unnamable, unobservable, the force-field
upon which 2 opposing armies meet.

It is the neutralizing force; when the battle ends
and both sides have withdrawn, the field
remains; it will be plowed, seeded, and

the grain harvested to make bread.

82

**"When armies are evenly matched,
the one with compassion wins."** (69. ii)

An army without virtue cannot,
in the long term, succeed; shame
will overcome it, not force of arms;

its generals are cruel and give rise
to tyrants, its privates rape both
the Mother and Her offspring;

they lay waste the land and pillage
the common stores, all
for want of virtue. The army with virtue

does only what is necessary,
no more; its excesses will be tempered
by compassion for the vanquished and

love for the Mother who nurtures us all:
absent the love of the Mother
locusts swarm, drought destroys the crops and

famine lays waste the villages and fields.

83

"The Sage dresses plainly." (70)

My Master wears a beggar's clothes,
those used and wrinkled cast-offs
which others scorned for something better;

He grows His hair long, then longer until
it hangs in dreadlocks to His butt and
He does all the driving, no matter

how tired He is or how hard He has worked.
People looking at Him would think
He was the hired help, yet

they are drawn to Him despite His
clever disguise because He cannot hide
the lightning hidden within the thundercloud.

Though He is barefoot and dust-covered, still
those with eyes to see recognize the King
by His erect carriage and fierce gaze:

though clouds cover the sky, still the Sun breaks through.

84

"Knowing ignorance is strength." (71) (Gia-Fu Feng)

The fool believes he knows and
trouble follows him
as the cart follows the Ox;

the needy follow him and
shower him with praise, thus
he believes himself wise;

the weak always insist
that they know, but
real strength arises in one

who knows his ignorance and
places all praise and reliance
on the Law to show him the Way;

knowing nothing, he remains always
a beginner, trusts the Law to speak
and act for him and his strength lies

in the faith that the Law will never fail.

85

**"Only when we are sick of our sickness
shall we cease to be sick."** (71. ii)

We remember ourselves and observe ourselves;
fever by blister by bloody scab,
heave and vomit and bloat,

foul wind and vaporous weeping,
we observe ourselves.
But before we have had enough,

we have to see every foulness in others
is manifest in ourselves, in thought
or emotion or outright action it is

all there; thus a certain shame
roots deep, sprouts, blooms as Remorse;
Conscience flowers, the balm upon the wound

of birth, the physician come to heal
the sickness of "myself." Conscience is the
Holy nurse in the fever-ward, that which is

deeply stirred, but untouched, by the plague.

"Do not despise the conditions of your birth." (72)

Through the blood-rent veil, the dark passage,
the terrible shock of ripped-and-torn,
through the fearful loss of the womb-wet world

we all came, every fur-bearing thing: into what?
Does it matter if there was nothing to greet you
but sorrow and fear, or the sweet thin stream

from the ripened breast? Still, we all came.
Now we get the rough moist clay, the raw stuff
from which we shape the vessel

of our longing and our desire.
Those who find the Way observe themselves,
this rude clay pot turning upon the wheel

of "myself"; they remember themselves, the pot
placed among the blowing grasses, worn by
wind and rain; what remains is a sturdy vessel

that can hold water without leaking.

87

"[Heaven's way] is not summoned, yet it appears." (73)

On the day my daughter's marriage
entered the crisis which
would lead to her separation,

we all were troubled, sorely upset
by the apparent difficulties when,
all of a sudden, out of nowhere and

with no reasonable explanation,
the little silver wedding bell
which hung over my desk,

given to us at her wedding,
fell on my desk. One moment
it was not there, the next it was.

The Tao is like this, mysterious, unfathomable,
yet the signs of Its reassurance are everywhere:
be calm, be clear, all is well;

only good will come of this.

88

**"If you are not afraid of dying,
there is nothing you cannot achieve."** (74)

Bloody-knuckled, coal-dusted-black,
flat-faced Big John Ireland shoveled coal
off his truck, down the chute, into

our basement. We feared the coal dust,
had heard of it igniting, exploding; we
asked him about it. "Hell," he said,

"I was in the War, died a hundred times,
lived to shovel coal. What's to be afraid of?
Yr gonna die anyways, some way."

The wise live in the present,
shovel coal, die each shovelful,
turn, live to shovel the next load.

Fear of death is refusal to live, to trust love,
believing the lie of tomorrow, mind's projection.
Big John Ireland slammed the chute door,

climbed into his truck, disappeared.

89

"There is always a lord of death." (74. ii) (07/22/2013)

Today my dear friend Mars met up with the Lord of Death:
"Hoka-Hey!" the Lakota say; it means
"It's a good day to die!"

You know Death is stalking you,
you know Death has its eye on you,
you know Death owns this world and

everything in it except love: love is
not of this world, it is of the dimension
of the present, a present-phenomenon only,

so why do you tarry, what do you fear,
what are you waiting for? Come home,
return to the Mother-Love and rest

in Her clear light where the Lord of Death
cannot find you; give all to the Mother and
She will show you the Way through the Valley

of the Shadow of Death. Fear no evil.

90

"The limb that does not bend, breaks in the wind." (76)

The Way is ever-changing,
never fixed, yet
a thousand years from now

one who follows the Way
will recognize others on the path.
The mind fixes, it names,

it categorizes, it rigidifies and
it calls this strength, yet
nothing rigid can last.

When the Earth trembles,
that which is rigid falls;
in a high wind, the tree

which does not bend is broken.
The Way adapts itself to the times:
though its form constantly changes,

still it is always the same.

"Return injury with kindness." (79)

Jesus said, "Be ye kind."
This is teaching simple enough
to be understood by little children,

like us.
He also said, "If a man should
strike you on one cheek,

turn the other cheek."
Peter asked Him, "Is it enough
to do this 7 times?" "No," He said,

"70 times 7," by which He meant
that there is no end to the practice
of returning injury with kindness.

The wise know kindness to be
the Supreme Way, the invisible suffering
that moves one from considering self only,

to that emptiness which considers others only.

92

**"[The wise] enjoy the labor of their hands,
and don't waste time inventing labor-saving machines."** (80)

In the boneyard, a man with a backhoe digs a grave that once
he dug by hand in 4 or 5 hours; now he is done in 20 minutes
and he is not tired, his hands aren't calloused, he no longer
 works

with his body, he doesn't get dirty.
When a man works with a machine, beyond what his body
alone can do, he becomes dangerous. Now he is able

to bring mountains down, change the course of rivers,
level whole forests and fish the oceans to exhaustion.
A man working with his body alone knows his limits

and his place, but give him a machine and now he needs
Conscience and humility or he will do more harm
than good; he will behave recklessly,

smitten by a false sense of power
because he can fell a mighty Oak in less than an hour.
Either he loves all things for their dignity and grace,

or beauty disappears from the world without a trace.

93

**"Although they live within sight of their neighbors…
they leave each other in peace…"** (80. ii)

Good neighbors know what their business is,
and how to mind it: they will come
on the running with blanket and bucket

if you've set the house on fire,
but if you're drunk and naked
in the backyard after dark

they're wise enough to say, "Fuck it,"
and trust that when they go off half-baked
and do some crazy shit like build an ark

in their backyard, you'll wander to the fence,
say, "Looks like rain," even if the Sun is quite intense,
and mind your own damn business.

Frost knew a good fence helped, and wine
or good weed makes for good relations.
If the Way was what governed among nations,

armed men would never cross the boundary line.

94

"True words are not beautiful." (81)

Plain and simple is the Way,
thus the mind rejects it;
the mind exults in its restless play,

so the fool is enamored of it.
The scholar will brag and brag
like an ass before the hay,

hoards knowledge and protects it,
fights to have the final say.
The philosopher argues how many whores

can dance on the head of his prick,
never ventures out of doors,
the Sunlight makes him sick.

But the wise rest by their hovel
after working all day with a shovel,
and eat their gruel with a spoon

while howling at the Moon.

Epilogue

Having known the children...

"Having known the children, we should go back and hold onto the Mother." (52. ii)

She who knows herself
knows the other
as herself and therefore

knows the universe
in a grain of sand; she ceases
to follow the restless mind

as it travels endlessly from the past
to the future, leaving in its wake
a multitude of sorrows,

the orphaned children of fear.
Like a prodigal child, she tires
of her restless wandering; her desires

exhausted, she longs for her home
in the present; humbled, she is embraced.
Coming home to the present is called

Returning to the Mother.

Bibliography

Dyer, Wayne. *Change Your Thoughts—Change Your Life: Living the Wisdom of the Tao.* Carlsbad, Calif.: Hay House, 2007.

Feng, Gia-Fu. *Tao Te Ching* by Lao Tsu. New York: Vintage Books/Random House, 1972.

Hamill, Sam. *Tao Te Ching: A New Translation.* Boston: Shambhala, 2005.

Star, Jonathan. *Tao Te Ching: The Definitive Edition.* New York: Jeremy P. Tarcher/Penguin, 2001.

About the Artists

Doris Martha Kessler Krieckhaus (1936–2015) was born in Stein am Rein, Switzerland. The youngest of eight children, she spent her adult life raising a family, traveling, and creating beauty through a variety of textile arts and crafts. Talented in drawing and painting from an early age, she explored Cubism and Modernism in her early twenties, but it was in her fifties when living in Taipei, Taiwan that she discovered a deep love of Chinese Classical painting. Her teachers declared that she was unusually gifted in this genre, especially for a westerner. In her years of retirement in the Colorado mountains she continued to paint this way, studying the *Tao Te Ching*, and living a life of simple contemplation and enjoyment of nature. **Cover Art, *Return to the Mother*; Plate 1, *Trailing Flowers and Fish* and Plate 2, *Migrating Birds***

Simona Sasarman has a degree in architecture from the Architecture Institute, Bucharest, Romania. She is a painter, graphic artist and theatrical set designer. Her artwork has been exhibited in Romania, Canada and France, and is part of private collections in Romania, France, England, Germany, Italy, Canada and USA. She lives in Bucharest, and is the mother of a twelve-year-old daughter. Simona writes: "I believe in unity, diversity, proportions, contrast, balance and surprise. I believe you can, just as life does, put together things however different from each other, and you can express the truth, however painful it might be, according to these rules. You just take the marker called 'fine arts' and underline things you want other people to see." **Plate 3,** *Untitled*

Michelle Meaux, born and raised in Paris in the 1960s, is a French mystic, poet and painter living in Dordogne, land of the famous Lascaux caves where early humans of that part of the world attempted to speak of what they saw. After many years in the United States, living in Colorado and Arizona, and translating spiritual authors as a way of service, she is training herself as a muralist and continues to feed her work as a writer and poet on what she understands of the dynamics between Intention and Matter, Heaven and Earth. **Plate 4,** *Side 2*

Sally Zell is a fairly new artist. After (nearly) raising her children, and learning a thing or two in the process, she began studying art the old-fashioned way as an apprentice. Her mentor is Preston Jackson, Professor Emeritus of the School of the Art Institute of Chicago. Her work as a doula and prenatal massage therapist/instructor have fed her love of the subject matter of pregnancy, labor and birth. **Plate 5,** *Still Life;* **Plate 6,** *Crowning Glory*

Denise Incao, born in Columbus, Georgia in 1966, spent her young life roaming forests, playing in gardens, sailing and exploring the barrier island beaches of Northern Florida. In 1995, she graduated cum laude with a BFA (Sculptural Ceramics) from Auburn University in Alabama. While building a respectable representation at galleries and museums in the southeast, she also created and directed various ceramics programs for schools and camps in Alabama, Tennessee and North Florida, and conducted adult classes and private lessons. After moving to Arizona in 1998, Denise continues these same pursuits in her home studio in Paulden, while teaching children and adults to "speak through clay." Denise is currently completing her master's degree in Expressive Eco-psychology and is designing programs that fuse nature immersion and expressive arts experiences. **Plate 7,** *Kuan Yin;* **Plate 8,** *Sleeping Woman*

Jocelyn Del Rio: "I do art for two main reasons: One is the sheer sensual pleasure of feeling my hands on different natural materials, caressing and manipulating them: the pleasure of seeing color appear, change, take on a life of its own as it relates to its placement whether intentional or accidental; the pleasure of witnessing the way in which a stroke takes on form, which in turn becomes narrative; the pleasure of using my whole body as a means to create or translate what I imagine and perceive into something tangible. The second reason is a fascination with humanity's relationship with itself and with nature. I am inspired by archetypical themes and experiences; inspired by the moments and movements which are unique each time they occur and yet timeless and universal.

"With this passion for the creative, aesthetic, human endeavor, I paint, sculpt, make paper and jewelry, plant trees and gardens, recover burnt-out land and build houses. My masterwork has been raising a family of five children. All this in México, both city and country, where I have deep roots." **Plate 9,** *Ixtlaccihuatl;* **Plate 10,** *The Sleeping Woman Must Give Birth;* **Plate 11,** *Cihuateteo;* **Plate 12,** *Mayahuel*

Other Hohm Press Books by Red Hawk

SELF OBSERVATION ~ THE AWAKENING OF CONSCIENCE
An Owner's Manual
by Red Hawk

This book is an in-depth examination of the much needed process of "self" study known as self observation. It offers the most direct, non-pharmaceutical means of healing the attention dysfunction which plagues contemporary culture. Self observation, the author asserts, is the most ancient, scientific, and proven means to develop conscience, this crucial inner guide to awakening and a moral life.

This book is for the lay-reader, both the beginner and the advanced student of self observation. No other book on the market examines this practice in such detail. There are hundreds of books on self-help and meditation, but almost none on self-study via self observation, and none with the depth of analysis, wealth of explication, and richness of experience that this book offers.

Paper, 160 pages, $14.95   ISBN: 978-1-890772-92-5

SELF REMEMBERING ~ THE PATH TO NON-JUDGMENTAL LOVE
A Practitioner's Manual
by Red Hawk

This companion piece to the author's previous book *Self Observation* offers detailed practical guidelines that allow one to know *with certainty* when one is Present and Awake. It details the objective feedback mechanisms available to everyone for attaining this certainty: Am I awake *now*? How do I know? Sincere readers will find invaluable help in answering these two questions.

Paper, 258 pages, $19.95   ISBN: 978-1-935387-92-3

To Order: 800-381-2700
Or visit our website at www.hohmpress.com

Other Hohm Press Books by Red Hawk

THE WAY OF POWER
by Red Hawk

"This is such a strong book. Red Hawk is like Whitman: he says what he sees…" —the late William Packard, editor, *New York Quarterly*.

"Red Hawk is a true poet whose work has strong, credible feelings and excellent timing." —Richard Wilbur, U.S. Poet Laureate and Pulitzer Prize winner.

"This collection continually surprises with insights that sometimes stop the breath." —Miller Williams, winner of 1995 Academy Award of the Academy of American Poets.

Paper, 96 pages, $10   ISBN: 978-0-934252-64-5

THE ART OF DYING
by Red Hawk

Red Hawk's poetry cuts close to the bone whether he is telling humorous tales or indicting the status-quo throughout the culture. Touching upon themes of life and death, power, devotion and adoration, these ninety new poems reveal the poet's deep concern for all of life, and particularly for the needs of women, children and the earth.

"An eye-opener; spiritual, native, populist. Red Hawk's is a powerful, wise, and down-home voice." —Gary Snyder

Paper, 132 pages, $12   ISBN: 978-0-934252-93-5

To Order: 800-381-2700
Or visit our website at www.hohmpress.com

Other Hohm Press Books by Red Hawk

WRECKAGE WITH A BEATING HEART
by Red Hawk

"Red Hawk's work puts us all in the line-up…We're all guilty, and Red Hawk himself is standing next to us."—Hayden Carruth, winner of the National Book Award, 1996.

This collection of over 250 new poems is Red Hawk's magnum opus, revealing the enormous range of his abilities in both free verse and sonnet forms. Red Hawk views the world with compassion tinged by outrage. He speaks with eloquence and raw power about all that he sees, including sex, death, hypocrisy and war as well as his own failures, and his life-altering remorse of conscience.

Paper, 300 pages, $16.95   ISBN: 978-1-890772-50-5

MOTHER GURU
Savitri Love Poems
by Red Hawk

A collection of refined devotional poetry in the tradition of Hafiz and Rumi. The author is an unabashed disciple of a great contemporary Master, Mister Lee Lozowick (1943–2010), and is willing to bare that discipleship in poetry written as prayer, expressly for and with his guru in mind and heart. These are poems of a truly broken heart. *Mother Guru* is a guidebook to the student-teacher relationship that offers inspiration and a call to profound honesty to the sincere seeker of any mystical tradition.

Paper, 208 pages, $19.95   ISBN: 978-1-935387-84-8

Other Titles of Interest from Hohm Press

GRACE AND MERCY IN HER WILD HAIR
Selected Poems to the Mother Goddess by Ramprasad Sen
Translated by Leonard Nathan and Clinton Seely

Ramprasad Sen, a great devotee of the Mother Goddess, composed these passionate poems in 18th-century Bengal, India. His lyrics are songs of praise or sorrowful laments addressed to the great goddesses Kali and Tara, guardians of the cycles of birth and death.

Paper, 120 pages, $12   ISBN: 978-0-934252-94-2

NOBODY SON OF NOBODY
Poems of Shaikh Abu-Saeed Abil-Kheir
Renditions by Vraje Abramian

Anyone who has found a resonance with the love-intoxicated poetry of Rumi must read the poetry of Shaikh Abil-Kheir. This renowned, but little known Sufi mystic of the 10th century preceded Rumi by over two hundred years on the same path of annihilation into God. This book contains translations and poetic renderings of 195 short selections from the original Farsi, the language in which Abil-Kheir wrote.

These poems deal with the longing for union with God, the desire to know the Real from the false, the inexpressible beauty of creation when seen through the eyes of Love, and the many attitudes of heart, mind and feeling that are necessary to those who would find the Beloved, The Friend, in this life.

Paper, 104 pages, $12.95   ISBN: 978-1-890772-08-6

To Order: 800-381-2700
Or visit our website at www.hohmpress.com

About the Author

Red Hawk was a Hodder Fellow at Princeton University, and currently teaches at the University of Arkansas at Monticello. His other books are: *Self Remembering: The Path to Non-Judgmental Love, A Practitioner's Manual* (Hohm Press, 2015); *Mother Guru: Savitri Love Poems* (Hohm Press, 2014); *Self Observation: The Awakening of Conscience: An Owner's Manual* (Hohm Press, 2009); *Raven's Paradise* (Bright Hill Press, 2010) winner 2008 Bright Hill Press poetry award, *Journey of the Medicine Man* (August House), *The Sioux Dog Dance* (Cleveland State University) nominated for the 1992 Pulitzer Prize in poetry; *The Way of Power* (1996); *The Art of Dying* (1999); and *Wreckage With a Beating Heart* (Hohm Press, 2005). He has published in such magazines as *The Atlantic, Poetry,* and *Kenyon Review.* He has given readings with Allen Ginsberg (1994), Rita Dove (1995), Miller Williams (1996), Tess Gallagher (1996), and Coleman Barks (2005), and more than seventy solo-readings in the United States.

Red Hawk is available for readings, lectures and workshops. He may be contacted at 824 N. Hyatt, Monticello, Arkansas, 71655; or via e-mail at: moorer@uamont.edu

About Hohm Press

Hohm Press is committed to publishing books that provide readers with alternatives to the materialistic values of the current culture, and promote self-awareness, the recognition of interdependence, and compassion. Our subject areas include parenting, transpersonal psychology, religious studies, women's studies, the arts and poetry. Our affiliate, Kalindi Press, publishes the Family and World Health Series for parents and children, and other adult books, primarily in the fields of health and nutrition.

Contact Information: Hohm Press, PO Box 4410, Chino Valley, Arizona, 86323; USA; 800-381-2700, or 928-636-3331; email: hppublisher@cableone.net

Visit our websites at:
www.hohmpress.com
www.kalindipress.com
www.familyhealthseries.com